A
CHILD
IN
RUINS

collected poems

José Luís Peixoto

translated by Hugo Dos Santos

selected by the author and translator

writ large press
los ángeles

A Child In Ruins
by José Luís Peixoto
translated by Hugo Dos Santos

Copyright © 2016 José Luís Peixoto
joseluispeixoto.com

Translation Copyright © 2016 Hugo Dos Santos
hugodossantos.com

Printed in the United States of America.
ISBN: 978-0-9814836-9-6

layout and design by Winona Leon

writ large press, los ángeles
www.writlargepress.com

CONTENTS

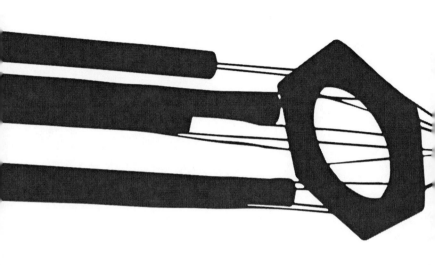

THE
CHILD
IN
RUINS

ARS POETICA

the poem has no more than the sound of its meaning,
the letter p is not the first letter in the word poem,
the poem is sculpted of senses and that is its form,
poem is not read poem, it is read bread or flower, it is read fresh
herb and your lips, it is read smile spread across a thousand
trees or sky of daggers, threat, it is read fear and blind
search, it is read child's hand or you, mom, who sleep
and made me born of you to be words that are
not written, it is read country and sea and forgotten sky and
memory, it is read silence, yes, so often, poem is read silence,
place that isn't uttered and that means, silence of your
sweet girlish stare, silence on sunday between conversations,
silence after a kiss or a fearless flower, silence
of you, dad, who died in everything only to exist in this quiet
poem, who can deny it? who write always and always, in
secret, inside of me and inside of all who suffer.
the poem is not the black ink pen, it is not this voice,
the letter p is not the first letter of the word poem,
the poem is when i could sleep late on summer
vacation and the sun entered through the window, the poem is
where i was happy and where i so often died, the poem is when i didn't
know the word poem, when i didn't know the
letter p and ate toast made in the kitchen in the
backyard, the poem is here, when i raise my eyes from the paper
and let my hands touch you, when i know, without rhymes
and without metaphors, that i love you, the poem will be when children
and birds rebel and, until then, it will be always and everything.
the poem knows, the poem understands itself and, to itself, never calls
itself poem, to itself, never writes itself with a p, the poem inside
itself is perfume and smoke, it is a boy who runs across an orchard to

hug its father, it is the exhaustion and the feeling of liberty, it is
everything i want to learn if what i want to learn is everything,
it is your stare and what i imagine of your stare, it is the loneliness and
regret, it is not libraries burning with verses told because those are
libraries burning with verses told and that is not the poem, it is not
the root of a word we think to know because we can only
know what we own and we own nothing, it is not a
clod of dirt singing anthems and stretching walls between
the verses and the world, the poem is not the word poem
because the word poem is a word, the poem is the
salty meat within, it is a stare lost in the night on the
rooftops in the hours when everyone sleeps, it is the last
memory of a drowning victim, it is a nightmare, anguish, hope,
the poem has no stanzas, it has a body, the poem has no verses,
it has blood, the poem is not written with letters, it is written
with grains of sand and kisses, petals and moments, screams and
uncertainties, the letter p is not the first letter of the word poem
the word poem exists in order not to be written like i exist
in order not to be written, not to be understood, not even by
myself, even if my meaning is in all the places where
i exist, the poem is me, my hands in your hair,
the poem is my face, that i don't see, and that exists because
you see me, the poem is your face, i don't know how to write
the word poem, me, i only know its meaning.

when it was time to set the table, we were five:
my father, my mother, my sisters
and me. then, my older sister
married. then, my younger sister
married. then, my father died. today,
when it is time to set the table, we are five,
except my older sister who is
at her home, except my younger
sister who is at her home, except my
father, except my widowed mother. each one
is an empty place at this table where
i eat alone. but they will always be here.
at the time to set the table, we will always be five.
as long as one of us is alive, we will always
be five.

even if you are there and you are there and
i am here we will always be in
the same place if we close our eyes
you will always be you and you who will teach me
to swim we will always be us under
the warm july sun and the tenuous veil
of our silence will always be
yours and your and my smile falling
and screaming of happiness upon diving
into the water upon looking for a hug that
doesn't need to be given will
always be yours and your and my
wet hair in the soft
breathing of the vines always yours
and your and my hands that don't
need to be held to still
feel that you are there and you are there and
i am here we will always be
together in this sunny july afternoon
swimming under the serene glide of
the pigeons in the shallow pond of
our garden always in the fresh pond
of the garden that was built for us
so that in life we could be
sister and sister and brother forever

there is the confined silence surrounding you
and yet your skin is the silence
there is the night that entered into you
and yet inside you isn't where
the children fall asleep it is where the blind
lose themselves it isn't where there is moon and stars
it is where the darkness doesn't wish to be so dark
you exist and you alone are your absolute emptiness
a man is the men who accompany him

this was the year you were born
and this year is prolonged its
months so long for you
this was the year that made you born
and you arrived at its breast like
a boat heavy with roses
a boat without rudder or oars
that arrives in the serene strength of the river
and in the strength of a day far too
strong in life in my life
in the life of your mother who
brought you like a perfumed boat
of petals coming down the river
a life far too strong and
being born and arriving in the exact
day this year you were born
for us for days and years
of distant auroras and nights
days long being born like
your child's smile
teaching us what we forgot in
growing teaching us to smile
again in life in your
life that has begun and stretches across
this year without night without source
where you arrived like a boat of
roses in the first morning
light

you shape of man person
were hurled upon the earth like
a top in the hands of children
i don't know i don't know perhaps
like a spontaneous flower
on the surface of the world
like many flowers on my
skin or in my chest
or inside my open eyes
or inside all of me
i don't know i don't know perhaps
you breeze between unintelligible
topics breeze in the
empty space between the
mysteries of a time
younger than me and
passing me leaving me or
i don't know i don't know perhaps
like a time of innocence
or one sole innocence on your
stare suspending the sky on my
skin or in my chest
or inside my open eyes
or inside all of me

death is this pen that isn't my fingers.
blade, meeting the walls, exploding.
a man
invisible in a field.
bodies of birds exploded in plain flight,
the words silenced inside of screams,
and that too is death.

even if spring and the children,
the books will piously cry resolute tears
and other thistles that will never be my eyes.
and if there are clouds, yes there will be,
an abyss will be resuscitated in my arms that
won't be the abyss of my arms,
and that will be death.

death: written, tree trunks
impossible to read.
a man
invisible in a field.
a day longer than a month, a year,
and agitating storms inside of shadows,
like a mystery.

i see in my handwriting the steps of my destiny.
that big house with a yard and chickens
dying cyclically. the sad mallows
in hopeless flower beds. and in each stanza
sitting before the landscape, the poem singular and final.
the women drag the afternoons through the verses, like
memories burning in all the nights of my life.
who can forget the afternoons, if the branches on the orange trees
were unforgettable? each word possesses a handful of that
infinite yard.

the fruit bowl on the kitchen table is blood on the poem.
my destiny was confined, and a destiny is forever.
the light crosses my outstretched hands
that shows the dust dancing in the air. i answer so many things to
the silverware in the drawer.

voices arrive that never left. faces arrive
that i dream when i wake up suddenly, crying. now,
you're the man of the house, they said. and there was no house any more.

a year passes for mom, like the hours pass for children who
still play on an imaginary street. innocent mom
and humiliated by the sky and the stars, by the dogs barking
in the distance, by the women whitewashing the walls, by the bells
that call us and by the road to the cemetery. mom,
life multiplied, as if your body ripped and the flesh
was the soil and the words, and the bones were the branches of the
orange trees and the words.

luckily, there are the verses, last hiding place of purity.
because destiny are the verses and the pigeons who cross
the sky in circles that always return.

my sisters sow thoughts in the absolute
darkness of the mornings. this is the present day, this is the
present hour. now, in this instant, on this last letter,
rests the weight of your hair. our dreams
cross the window and stretch across the floor, come from the sky,
draw us shadows near old and useless
bodies. we bathe. the water. the water. our
dreams dissolve slowly where we forget them.

i am in the house where the memories are sitting on chairs
to eat dinner on invisible plates. that's a beautiful portrait.
that jar was bought at the october fair. that
book has words that don't mean anything.

there is a fruit bowl on the table where daily my mother serves
my destiny. there is a hallway daily recalling
the populated loneliness. there is paper and verses. there is all
i don't say, that i don't know how to say, that is in my handwriting,
that is neatly organized on the leaves of the abandoned yard of so many
            autumns.
there is a table, an unlit fireplace, the hands, a grave
alone in the cemitery, the eyes, the bones, my skin and the hours
written in the impossible future.

when i was born. i hoped that life.
would bring me. the soil. when i was born.
i hoped that life. would bring me.
the trees. and the birds. and the children.
when i was born. i had the world. entire.
after the eyes. after the fingers.
and i didn't understand. i didn't understand. anything.
i never imagined. when i was born. that life.
when i was born. was already the darkness. the darkness.
where i was. when i was born.

i am lying on my absence
like i could be lying if i existed.
tomorrow the waves will imitate me on the shore.

between me and my silence there are shouts of booming colors
and naturally occurring magic cut from my dreams.
i am the bed where i lie, different every night,
i am the shrill smile of the birds in the entirety of the sky,
i am the sea, the old ocean opening its mouth in a
cave that frightens children and men who know
the world. i am what i shouldn't be and i laugh, laugh,
laugh, because i am pure, because i am a bit of happiness,
because a thousand hands and ten thousand fingers run over my body
and kiss me. between me and my silence there is a
confusion of misconceptions that i don't understand and don't allow.
i am arrogant, because i am from the country that invented
arrogance. i am wretched. what do i know? i am a traveler
with my destiny traced out, like the smoke from this cigarette that
vanishes undecided and has already forgotten where it came from. and i
        laugh,
laugh, laugh, lost and heartless, with dirty teeth and almost
sick, because this hope is mine and so is this yearning
to be born each morning, in each face, in each
lit match, in each star. i laugh, laugh, laugh, because love
is mine and so is mourning and hunger and all the things
that make this life that i don't understand and follow.
i am a breathing man feeling each stone,
i am a breathing man feeling each mountain,
i am a breathing man feeling each grain of sand.
disorderly, i am someone who is me without knowing,
between me and my silence there is a misunderstanding
carved in the flowers and in the clouds, i laugh, laugh, laugh,
i am life and the sun illuminating me.

spring has arrived before its time in this room.
its light comes in through the window and that is what i write.
the cigarette smoke, so opposed to spring,
reminds me that i wished to be something else somewhere else,
maybe a ship i wanted to be, maybe a breeze.
i know that i need only write it for it to happen but i lost
the strength to say it at the moment and the blank page
burned before me, lit by a distant god.
spring has arrived illuminated and, i confirm in my pocket
watch and on the wall calendar, it is still winter
and álvaro de campos tells me i am nothing, álvaro
de campos tells me i will never be anything, tells me i can't
want to be anything, and i am alone and far from
all of those who make the streets by walking,
and the only resemblance we have is smoking
cigarettes that will kill us before our time,
i on purpose, them without wanting to, we will die
perhaps without noticing that we died many times
and that we take layers of mourning overlapping our skin.
spring has arrived and it didn't bring me any more than
the knowledge that all you honest men pass
in the living room outside my open window and, closed,
haven't yet heard the voice of álvaro de campos today
because the silence of your words prevents you
from hearing his words in your own.
i smoke cigarettes endlessly and my stare
draws smoke in the light and my fingers release ashes
on the first demands of spring.
i dreamt everything, napoleon nero, i dreamt everything and lost
everything in the empty arms of that boy who is

rocking another boy, ah, if i could sacrifice you
boy that i was and all of your dreams of not
knowing anything but dreaming, if i could make you into
the memory of one who died before birth and
who remained on the verge of being able to be everything.
yes, spring, yes, spring has arrived along with the
solemn aggravation of the doves flying sadly.
the cigarettes burn between my fingers and i am this
figure of smoke moving heavily in the air of the living room,
this large body of smoke coming undone and growing
each time denser each time more tiring
and remembering so many faces i want to forget
and you, lídia diotima desdemona dulcineia, when
your face if winter denies your expression,
if this living room is just the darkness of me not being anything,
you will arrive from the street and bring on your face all the smiles
and all the stares of those with whom i share the misfortune
of belonging to the species labeled human that i have renounced,
you will force me to embrace you touching with revulsion all those
i despise like i despise the plague and leprosy,
i won't tell you i can't want to be anything, my hands
will become two gray silences shrinking inside
the walls of smoke killing me killing you killing me,
two assassin hands wrapping around your neck,
ripping me apart and exposing me finally before this light.
it's spring it's spring and i want desperately to die.
i am nothing, i will never be anything, i can't want to be anything.
i smoke, and my pain is that it's too late to surrender while winning,
my pain is knowing what i created today at the beginning
of saturday mornings, in the first days of spring
of me being the world and the sun of me dreaming this day.
my pain is this spring that is born and shows me
that winter wedged itself permanently within me.

since i don't have a place in the silence where seagulls die,
i say farewell to the ocean and allow the sky to recognize me.
maybe serenity can be my hands as a
breeze above the earth and above the naked skin of a woman.
that day, hopefully tomorrow, may arrive and i will be sleeping.
today, i am a bit of something, i am the salt water
that remains on the waves that reject and expel everything
on the beach. the seagulls fly over my living body. my
submerged hair invites the morning silence, rays of sunlight cross
the sea turned luminous water. here, i am alive and i am someone
far away.

it was the stars, wanderer,
the map you could not decipher
so you will continue and continue
lost forever.

i am astonished when people, by chance and almost always
without motive, tell me they don't know what love is.
i know exactly what love is. love is knowing
there is a part of us that has ceased to belong to us.
love is knowing we will forgive everything to that part
that is not ours. love is being weak.
love is being afraid and wanting to die.

i ask if i can say your name to a flower
flower your name whispered petal by petal
letter by letter a flower mutilated on the earth

we climbed the eiffel tower

slowly on the elevator
softly on the lazy touch
of your soft voice
slowly on the steps
calm on the lazy echo
of your calm fingers
we climbed the eiffel tower

we climbed and found one another
in the certainty

paris spread out on the world
all alive grows stretches
across the entire surface of the world
that lives and runs in the streets
in the roads beneath
us inside our veins
in our heart pumping
light and paris in the night so
distant

we climbed

slowly a breeze
in your hair in my hands
slowly a breeze
on your skin in my hands

we climbed

paris is the immense shadow
of us

today there is no wind and i can see you more clearly
our son fell asleep in your arms
and you are the early morning fluvial stare that
stretches always to my skin and
touches it as if it were skin to touch and
really feel or had more value this skin
our son fell asleep in your portrait
today i don't suffer and i can tell you
about the fields of dry soil
that swallowed all the rain in the days that
passed the soil suspended beneath
our feet and i say peace say i who close
the simple love of your grandiose beauty
i say peace and the sky fans the gliding flight
of many birds simple and small
who will never be able to understand the grandiose
serenity of the sky our son fell asleep
on you and you and he are what i breathe this day
with no wind and for me i don't want more than
this frozen instant

i don't want to live any more. i am tired of lying.
i see your face frozen in a picture and the memory
i save of you is so different from the frightening reality of the pictures.
but i will not lie. i am tired of lying.
my life is also you, your face frozen in my memory.
my life is you and all the hands that held me and desired me,
all the lips that kissed me, all the tongues that drew figures
on my skin, all the teeth that bit me, all the voices that told me they loved
        me
and made me believe that. i don't want to lie any more. i am tired of lying.
you are almost nothing, but i don't want to and i won't pretend you never
        existed.

in the time we were happy it didn't rain.
we got up together, hugging the sun.
the mornings were an infinite sky. our love
was the mornings. in the time we were happy
the horizon could be touched with tips of our fingers.
the seas brought the end of the afternoon and we saw
more than one another's stares. we played
and we were happy children. sometimes i still
wait for you like i waited for you when you came
with the beautiful uniform of your innocence. it's been
so long since i've waited for you. so long since you've come.

give me some of your skin soil
you that don't ask me for anything and
appear to me at night dressed in
nakedness skin soil and open pathways that
allow me to know you give me some
of the silence you give me so that
in it i can tell you skin soil if at night
you appear to me illuminated with many
birds being born and flying being
born and flying silence skin soil
allow me to know you give me what
you give everyone and never gave except
to me skin soil you that give me
the gestures in my hands
the music of my words that
give me skin soil hide yourself
within me

i am here. this table. you are sitting on a couch that i can only imagine
you're wearing the lipstick i gave you and you smile for a man
who is thirty years older than you. around you everyone smiles. no one
        looks
at your skin with my eyes. the man tells you things and you smile always,
the man rests his hand on your leg, the man rests his hand on your
hair and doesn't know that, on a day that's since passed, only i could do so.
        you stand up
and the man stands up after you. you have on your finger the ring in the
        shape of a heart
that I gave you, you have around your neck the childhood necklace i gave
        you for your birthday. you smile.
i am here. this table. i close my eyes and see you shut the door to the room.

lately i can't sleep and i can't wake up. yesterday
pretty late at night in the hours when i can be even more
alone, i sat by the fire and recalled when we would sit
together on your grandmother's front step and to the people walking by
we were a couple. we shared conversations that were only ours and
sometimes we kissed. i sat by the fire and thought of your
body when i held you and thought that maybe in that moment
a man may be having pleasure inside you. today
i sat still with still hands, wtih a still face and
i remembered your skin so smooth, your pretty fingers,
your girlish eyes and i think that maybe in this moment
a man is having pleasure inside you.

all the love in the world was not enough because love serves for nothing.
there remain only
the papers and the sadness, remain only the bitterness and the cigarette
ash and death.
the sundays and the evenings we spent making plans were not enough
and were
too many because today they are like blood on my face, they are like
tears.
i know that we loved one another immensely and one day, when i no
longer find you
in each instant, in each hour, i will not deny that. i will never deny that i
loved you.
not even when i am lying, naked, on the sheets of another and she forces
me to say i love her
before i fuck her.

the boat moves forward without a destination.
the nights, the days, the boat moves forward without a destination.
the ocean is infinite.

when our bodies separated we looked at one another almost hoping for
        happiness.
i dressed slowly, the body being ridiculous. i said i hope that you meet a
        man
who loves you, and we both lowered our eyes for knowing that man does
        not exist.
we said goodbye. you remained forever lying naked on the bed, i left
        forever
in the night. we looked at one another for the last time and said goodbye
        without even knowing who we were.

pretending that everything is fine: the body ripped and dressed
in ironed clothes, remnants of flames inside
the body, desperate screams under the conversations: pretending
that everything is fine: you look at me and only you know: in the street
where our stares meet it is night: people
don't imagine: people are so ridiculous, so
deplorable: people talk and don't imagine: we
look at ourselves: pretending that everything is fine: the blood boiling
beneath the skin equal to the days before everything, storms of
fear on smiling lips: will i die?, i ask
inside of myself: will i die?, you look at me and only you know:
hot irons, fire, silence and rain that cannot be described:
love and death: pretending that everything is fine: having to smile: an
ocean that burns us, a fire that drowns us.

one day, when tenderness is the only rule of the morning,
i will wake up in your arms. your skin will be perhaps too pretty.
and the light will understand the impossible understanding of love.
one day, when the rain dries in the memory, when winter is
distant, when the cold answers slowly with the dragging voice
of an old man, i will be with you and birds will sing on our
windowsill. yes, birds will sing, there will be flowers, but none of that
will be my fault, because i will wake up in your arms and i will not say
even one word, not even the beginning of a word, in order to avoid spoiling
the perfection of happiness.

time, suddenly free through the streets and days,
like the wave of a storm dragging the world,
shows me how much i loved you before i met you.
it was your eyes, labyrinths of water, earth, fire, air,
that i loved while imagining i loved. it was your
your voice saying the words of life. it was your face.
it was your skin. before i met you, you existed in the trees
and in the hills and in the clouds that i saw at the end of the afternoon.
far from me, inside of me, you were the clarity.

THE HOUSE, THE DARKNESS

WORDS FOR MY MOTHER

mom, i'm sorry, i always hoped you would understand
the words i never said and the gestures i never made.
today i know that i only waited, mom, and waiting isn't enough.

for the words i never said, for the gestures you so often asked
of me and which i was never able to make, i want to ask your
forgiveness, mom, and i know that asking forgiveness isn't
enough.

sometimes, i want to tell you so many things that i can't.
the photograph where i am on your lap is the most
beautiful photograph i have. i like it when you're happy.

read this: mom, i love you.

i know and you know that i can always pretend that i didn't
write these words. yes, mom, i will pretend that
i didn't write these words, and you will pretend that you didn't
read them. we are like that, mom, but i know and you know.

WORDS

your hands, or your skin, or your lips.
your stare. your stare always reminds me that

or your hair, or the exact way how
your face. your face. or your body that
falls asleep where the wind hasn't forgotten to

or each of your words, words,
words in a language of impossible skies.

THE MOST BEAUTIFUL WOMAN IN THE WORLD

you look so beautiful today. when i say that new flowers
bloomed in the soil in the garden, i mean that
you look beautiful.

i enter the house, enter the room, open the wardrobe, open
a drawer, open a box that contains your gold
necklace.

between my fingers, i hold your fine gold necklace, as if
i touched the skin on your neck.

there is the sky, the house, the room, and you are within me.

you look so beautiful today.

your hair, forehead, eyes, nose, lips.

you are within something that is within all the
things, my voice nominates you to describe
beauty.

your hair, forehead, eyes, nose, lips.

up against the silence, within the world,
you look so beautiful is what i want to say.

LOVE

your face waiting for me. your face
smiling for my eyes. there exists a
clap of thunder over the mountain.

your hands are fine and fair. you see me
smile. breezes light the world ablaze.
i breathe the light on the redbud's leaves.

i enter the october hallways to
find an embrace in your eyes.
this day will always be today in memory.

today i understand the rivers. the age of the
rocks tells me profound words.
today i have your face within me.

this book. run a finger across the page, feel the paper
as if you were feeling the skin of my body, my face.

this book has words. forget the words for
moments. what we have to say can't be said.

feel the weight of this book. the weight of my hand on
yours. we hold hands when you hold this book.

don't ask me who i am. don't ask me anything.
i don't know how to answer all the questions of the world.

rest your lips on the page. rest your lips on
the paper. slowly, very slowly, we will kiss.

LOVE

when the instants of tomorrow accumulate on the
walls of the house, i rip the pages where i write you,
because i know that everything will be unnecessary, everything will
be fragile. when i imagine the sun that i may not be able to see,
i forget the walls and,

with such resolve,

i want you to be happy.

LOVE

there was so much time, your face and the horizon descended
in place of the morning. the children that walked past us
spoke of your small lips and of the days without hours.

it was your eyes that shined the first light of each
morning. the rooms where we slept embracing were
full of moments that passed slowly to eternity.

mom, i know you still keep one thousand stars on your lap.
i, so often, still believe that one thousand stars are
all the stars that exist.

THE BOOKS

on each page, your stare. on each mountain,
your voice. let me speak with you. i remember
so well everything you said to me.

the words exist. i want to find you
always, in each night, on the desk cluttered
with papers where i clutter our life.

on each page, the fields. on each mountain,
you calling me. the pages are, again,
the day i was born. i remember everything so well.

years pass over the words. the days exist.
i hold the books as if i held your voice
and, when someone utters your name, i keep answering.

mom, each word you taught me repeats your name one thousand times.

in the silence that precedes your voice, i am still
before its beauty.

if i reached out my arm, i would touch your lithe body.

but i could never touch your beauty. between me and
your beauty there is the impossible distance that divides
life from death.

DESCRIPTION OF A MARTYRDOM

threw him on the ground and the blades. cut off his arms
and, then, his legs. ripped his arms and his legs
from his body. yes, the blood.

left him alone and his body. reluctantly it rotted slowly.
the skin and the flesh rotting before the children and the innocence.
the flesh rotted to the bone.

the martyrdom was when she left. he looked at her. and couldn't
wave, couldn't say impossible words
like the word good-bye.

NOBODY

no place can be heard in the place where you don't exist.
here, there isn't even your forgetting. there are words
that don't deny you. we grew up expecting nothing from you.

if you are the silence, we don't know the silence. if you're
the loneliness, you're useless. what exists far from us isn't
our home. we support the walls of our home.

no time can forget the time that forgot you.
now, the music repeats other faces. the instants don't
remember you. the horizon tries to protect you from fear

if one day i could hold your face in my hands
the skin of your face growing older, if i could one day touch it
like i touch water from a spring, like i touch light.

it's a secret i will keep my entire life for not knowing how to say it.
the face,
your face submerged in innocence, mom.

EXPLANATION OF ETERNITY

slowly, time transforms everything in time.
hate is transformed in time, love
is transformed in time pain is transformed
in time.

the topics we consider most profound,
most impossible, most permanent and immutable,
are transformed slowly in time.

in and of itself, time is nothing.
the age of nothing is nothing.
eternity doesn't exist.
yet, eternity exists.

the instants of your eyes on me were eternal.
the instants of your smile were eternal.
the instants of your body of light were eternal.

you were eternal until the end.

THE INVASIONS

suddenly, the faces transformed themselves in blood.

suddenly, the blades crossed the flesh.

suddenly, the children died.

the end came slowly.

i am lying on my absence
like i could be lying if i existed.
tomorrow the waves will imitate me on the shore.

PAPER
DRAWER

PHOTOGRAPH OF SAN FRANCISCO

San Francisco is you and all the afternoons spent
on the couch, sitting or lying in all fashions,
in all directions. I don't hold resentment
of San Francisco and there will come a time when,
again, we will be able to spend a weekend
between beach umbrellas and the sun. California is not
eternal, but there is a certain type of silence that is
always sought and seldom discovered.
That is your luster, San Francisco. You will see, we will
have flowered shirts and we will know how to laugh
at everything. And, against all expectations, when
one of us is at death's door, the other will be there.

PHOTOGRAPH OF MADRID

Madrid will return always. We need years
to learn that which only happens with
the distance of years. That is why I can affirm
that Madrid will return always. I don't know what type
of understanding we found. Madrid and I don't
know each other well. We know the essential and
make up the rest. Both my life
and Madrid's life have had many forms.
Still, when we meet, we are
always the same name. We evaluate each other
through scars and minor marks of aging.
We don't establish goals, we are tired.
Madrid and I only want a bed, but,
if that isn't possible, we will be happy with the floor and,
if that isn't possible, we will be happy with an embrace.

PHOTOGRAPH OF COIMBRA

Coimbra is the city and the hope of Sunday afternoons.
An abandoned calendar in a coat pocket is Coimbra.
Coimbra are the developed photographs of an old roll,
forgotten in a drawer. And, at the same time, while we speak,
Coimbra exists and runs in the playground. There is air that is breathed
solely by Coimbra. There is a heart beating in its breast,
and that is a miracle of god that transcends god.

BIRTH CERTIFICATE

Portugal, I fill my mouth with this word, I chew it.
I fill out forms with the numbers of a date
when I weighed 8 pounds and 2 ounces.

Portugal is the name of people that phone one
another, that pass one another on the highway and
that say goodbye with the same syllable.

The day I was born is my mother with her eyelids
fainting over her eyes, thinking of labyrinths and
knitting them in the heart of her dreams.

Portugal and the day I was born mix without
losing their color, they are complimentary substances
on a microscope slide.

Portugal and the day I was born are twin brothers,
dressed the same, with family members
amusing themselves trying to distinguish us.

The day I was born is Portugal, a complete country,
but Portugal is much more than merely one day.
Portugal is the instant I was born

of me being the world and the sun of me dreaming this day.
my pain is this spring that is born and shows me
that winter wedged itself permanently within me.

ROADSIDE CROSSES

They are like sad shadows, they are like autumn.
You can look inside the roadside
crosses, they are like wells, they are like lost

sons. The roadside crosses are
covered by plastic flowers, dried, faded
by the light that, on the fields, plays with faces

and with memory. There exist lines traced between
the sky and the roadside crosses, they are the ones
that hold a part of the world, only their parents are
able to see them.

Now, while we speak of paper kites,
there they are, where they have always been.

The roadside crosses are different
from us because if we are the wind and pass,
the roadside crosses are also the wind,
but it's been a long time since they were able to arrive there.

When I grew tired of lying to myself,
I started to write a book of poetry.

I decided two hours ago, but it has been much
longer since I started to tire. The tiredness
is a skin gradual like autumn. Pause.

Rest slowly on the flesh, like the leaves
on the earth, and sink only to the bones,
like the leaves sink into the earth and touch
the dead and turn fertile by their side.

The city continues in the streets, the girls laugh,
but there is a secret that ferments in the silence.
It's the words, free, the books yet to be written,
that which will come with future seasons.

There is always hope at the end of the avenues.
But there are puddles on the sidewalks. There is cold,
there is tiredness, I decided two hours ago, autumn.

And my body doesn't want to lie, and that which
isn't my body, time, knows that
I have many poems to write.

Your idle lips were the night, the abyss
and the silence of idle waves meeting with
the rocks. Your face in my hands.
My fingers on your lips and the tenderness,
like the horizon, beneath my fingers.
My lips approaching your lips.
Your half-opened eyes, your eyes and
your lips approaching my lips
approaching your lips approaching
my lips, your lips.

When we stay like this, listening to ourselves and
speaking to ourselves, we are capable of discovering
much more than all of them, obedient and afraid.
Like here, like this, these words taking this
voice let us know we are together, even
when there isn't a room with these walls and
we can only doubt and doubt this truth.
We are together, even when we separate
through the streets and, within us, we are an army
of secrets, even when we hide from the
world that we desired and that we desire
indescontrollably, unincomparably, like a
silence that lies and lies and doesn't lie.

      We are together in the silence, despite this voice
heavy with these words, despite all the forms of
our bodies and of the drawings we are capable
of making with our stares. Our hands search one another
in the night, inside the turned out lights. Our hands,
ours, find one another now and they are invisible. We know
that our fingers have touched other fingers, touched
names and guitar chords. We know who we are.
We are many and we recognize ourselves. Like this,
like here, we await the morning, knowing that it
was us, together, that built it. We await
much more than the morning.   We have the
strength of forever, we learn the repudiation of
never again. The discipline is buried in what
isn't fear, it's strength, and it protects us, that
we protect ourselves. This voice, if they
can understand this voice, we will replace our

tongue. This voice is this room. This voice are the ways
we made on the margins of cities and of reasonable
arguments. The words are stones. The certainties
follow us and we slow to allow them to catch
us.   Now, we control bridges and
the mundane. Now, this voice is directed at your face.
Nothing is impossible. Not even the impossible
is impossible for us. We explain ourselves to one another
and, without anyone bothering us, we meet
always   like now, here, like this, like now,
here, like this

I have a thousand sisters to love without words.
I have that sister who walks leaning
on the walls and without a voice, have that sister of
hope, have that sister who undoes her
face when she cries. I have sisters covered
in the marble of statues, reflected in
lake water. I have sisters spread across
gardens. I have a thousand sisters who were born
before me so that, when I was born,
I would have a velvet bed. I thank with
love each of my sisters. They are one thousand
and each one has an aging face. My
thousand sisters are a thousand mothers I have.
The eyes of my sisters follow me with
kindness and, when they don't understand me,
it is because I don't understand myself.
I have a thousand sisters awaiting me always, with
silence to hear me and protect me
in winter. I have that sister who is a
girl who leaves home early to arrive early
at school and have that sister who is a
girl who leaves home early to arrive early
at school. I have sisters like music, like
music. I have a thousand sisters made of white.
I am brother to them all. I am the permanent
and relentless keeper of their peace.
I have to be happy for my sisters.
I have to be happy for my sisters.

Now, I no longer need them to like me.
Now, I have a thousand pieces of a puzzle, I have
a box full of loose clothes pins, two hands,
I have a house plant, I have branches
ready for winter, and so much silence,
I have so much silence, pockets empty and full,
bread, faith, sky, floor, sea, salt, sun, here and there,
I have there above all, an immense distance
made of stretched planes and eternity
because I walk slowly along the
roads, the horizon is too much when
I glide its entire distance without fear of
anything, merely fearless, courage is
an army at my side, I have the necessary
courage, I have a lake that reflects the
night and the moon when there is a moon, an entire
orchestra I have, the sound and the silence, I already said
the silence, I repeat it knowing who I am and what I
have, I have a paper drawer, I have
mountains of mountains, I have air, I have
time and I have a word that runs
in front of me, but that I can catch
and still use in the poem.

And love transformed into a different thing with the same name.
This is what mothers meant when they gave their daughters
advice and said: love comes later. This was the later.
A simple tenderness, almost painful, lots of silences,
all the hours of the day and a poem that dissolves within
me and that, slowly, faceless, disappears.

DISMANTLING A RIVER

I rip the stickers off the wall of our son's bedroom,
as if the electric kitchen knife crossed my arm.
I'm the one who erases his drawings from the wall. They're not scratches,
they're drawings. There are grease pencils scattered and broken on the
        floor.
After us, this address will have other names and patient letters
will arrive in the mailbox. Now, they are impossible to imagine,
like our yesterday will be impossible to imagine. It was little by little
that we got to merely the couch and the refuse and the stripped cabinets.
It was very late that we arrived at nights where I sleep
on the couch, on a blanket gifted by my mother or yours.
Finally, I have time to adjust my eyes to the shadows and evaluate
the devastation, waking with the cold air of the early morning, the
        forgetting,
and witnessing that blue hour where it is no longer night, but where
there is still a long way to go before day. I dump into the bottom of a bag
all that is in the drawer neither of us ever straightened up.
Around me, there are crates that serve to store the books,
they are already divided. I choose the place to rest my feet. We did
things in this empty room, we had thoughts, we learned
alphabets. All I have now is what I always had and, as if falling
helplessly in a bathtub, I proceed and continue my work,
as if hitting my head on the corner of a drawer,
I proceed and continue my work.

REHEARSAL

I was being just one part of me and you
were being just one part of you. The lights

were probable. I, whole, needed so badly
to hear the wonder that you said, in the exact way

that you said it, but you were being just
one part of you, because if you were unique

and complete, with the roots and scars,
with the postcards that you wrote in your mind

and never sent, you wouldn't speak like that.
Besides, I wouldn't remain silent merely listening to you.

If you were being you, there would be a noun
incorrectly pronounced, or incorrectly understood, and that single

and complete word could be yours or could
be mine if I was being me. That error

would be the first step. Then we would know
how to arrive at the old words that bruise.

And, despite having already written I needed so much
to hear the wonder that you said, I wouldn't be able

to admit that it was that simplicity I wanted,
and you wouldn't either, though it was that same

simplicity you wanted. And we would both have
the omnipotent certainty of knowing ourselves.

Luckily, none of this was needed because
I was being just one part of me,

you were being just one part of you
and the lights were probable, like reticence's.

DUSTING

As if yesterday and all the days before yesterday
had disintegrated above the shelves,

as if we could write words
on their ashes with the tip of a finger,

as if we had only to blow on them to see
their images anew, in a cloud.

WASHING THE DISHES

And destroying all the evidence of a night:
two glasses, two bodies, forks spooning

together, knives like repeated words.
And believing that the world is reborn in water.

The precise circumference of the plates, the absolute
color of white. And forgetting again.

José Luís Peixoto is one of Portugal's most acclaimed and bestselling novelists. He was born in 1974 in Galveias, in the region of Alentejo (Portugal). Since 2000, Peixoto has published ten titles, four novels, three fiction books, and three poetry collections. He is  a three-time winner of the Jovens Criadores Prize. His first novel, *Blank Gaze / The Implacable Order of Things*, won the José Saramago Literary Award in 2001. *Blank Gaze* was selected by Expresso as one of their ten best books of the decade. In 2007, his novel, *The Piano Cemetery*, won the Calamo Award for best translated novel in Spain. In 2012, Peixoto published *Dentro do Segredo, Uma Viagem na Coreia do Norte (Inside the Secret, a Journey in North Korea)*, his first work of nonfiction. Peixoto's poetry and short stories have appeared in a great number of anthologies in dozens of languages. All his novels have been internationally acclaimed and have been translated in twenty languages. He is also a heavy metal fan and in 2003, he set out on an unprecedented collaboration with the heavy metal band Moonspell that resulted in the 2013 collection of short stories, *Antidote*, published in translation in the US by Writ Large Press in 2013.

Hugo dos Santos is a Luso-American writer and translator. He is a Disquiet International fellow and his work has appeared in various publications in the U.S. and Europe. He lives in New Jersey.